FRUITFUL MARRIAGE

CULTIVATE VALUES, ESTABLISH VISION, AND BUILD AGREEMENTS ON A "WE" RETREAT

Be sure to get the complete
Fruitful Marriage Video Series
free by going to:

www.strongermannation.com/fruitful-marriage

These will be utilized throughout your "WE" Retreat.

FRUITFUL MARRIAGE: CULTIVATE VALUES, ESTABLISH VISION, AND BUILD AGREEMENTS ON A "WE" RETREAT

Copyright © 2024

Scriptures taken from the Holy Bible, New International Version®, NIV®. Copyright© 1973, 1978, 1984, 2011 by Biblica, Inc.™ Used by permission of Zondervan. All rights reserved worldwide. www.zondervan.com The "NIV" and "New International Version" are trademarks registered in the United States Patent and Trademark Office by Biblica, Inc.™

Published by Stronger Man Nation.

All rights reserved. No part of this publication may be reproduced in any form, stored in a retrieval system, or transmitted in any form by any means—electronic, mechanical, photocopy, or otherwise—without the prior permission of the publisher, except as provided by United Sates of America copyright laws.

This book is dedicated to Greg and Candy McPherson.
No one else has more passion about marriage and family than you.
Thanks, Mom and Dad.

CONTENTS

Introduction   1

BEFORE YOU GO

How It Works (Preparing for Your "WE" Retreat)   3
Pro Tips   4
Practical Encouragement for Moms   6
Our Prayer For You   8

ON YOUR "WE" RETREAT

Chapter 1 COVENANT   12
Chapter 2 VALUES   22
Chapter 3 VISION   32
Chapter 4 AGREEMENTS   42
Chapter 5 UNITY & ONENESS   52
Chapter 6 BUILDING AGREEMENTS   58

APPENDIX

Appendix A Bible Verses to Feed Your Roots   71
Appendix B 6 Critical Elements of a Godly Marriage   72

INTRODUCTION

"Therefore a man shall leave his father and his mother and hold fast to his wife, and they shall become **one flesh**."

Genesis 2:24

Over the years, we've talked with many couples who want to strengthen their marriage, but the practical question is always, "yeah, but what do we do?"

This guidebook and the Fruitful Marriage Video Series will provide you with a step-by-step facilitation of a "WE" Retreat. It will walk you through what to do before, during, and after the retreat. It gives you a structure to follow, questions that encourage dialogue, assessments to help you gauge where you're at, and assignments to complete together.

But the process is only as good as the energy you put into it. This guidebook won't do the hard work for you. It will, however, give you the tools necessary to build a strong marriage. We guarantee your marriage will become increasingly fruitful and sweet as a result of this focused time.

Marriage works because God designed it to work. Marriage also takes work, which is why we are so glad you're holding this resource.

The endgame is clarity, unity, purpose, power, and oneness. Experiencing that will require humbling yourselves, working together, communicating, thinking, praying, repenting, forgiving, talking, listening, reflecting, writing—all for the sake of living joyfully with a shared purpose.

In a phrase…you'll be farming your "WE."

Let's get to work.

Get the Fruitful Marriage Video Series to watch on your "WE" Retreat

BEFORE YOU GO

HOW IT WORKS
(Preparing for Your "WE" Retreat)

What is a "WE" Retreat?
In the simplest terms, a "WE" Retreat is a trip a husband and wife take to focus on their marriage. It creates the environment in which you can focus on your shared values, your marriage vision, and your agreements, and it can be a lot of fun.

How long do we need to plan for?
Ideally, 3-5 days. Any shorter and you might feel rushed and frustrated (experience talking here). But one day to focus on your marriage is better than none and can get you started. Our recommendation is to take a longer retreat once a year. Then, throughout the year, take quarterly, 48-hour check-ins to assess your progress and prune where needed.

Can we take our kids?
Sharon just said, "Heck no." Think torpedo into the side of a ship. Your kids are great, but this isn't about your kids. If you love them, you'll leave them home. You need "WE" time.

Practical Help: Enlist grandparents or church family. Exchange babysitting weekends with another couple. Tell them what you are doing. Ask them to help your marriage by caring for your kids.

Where should we go on our "WE" Retreat?
Anywhere that is not home. You have to get away or it doesn't count as a retreat. The physical separation is essential for mental freedom (especially for the wife). All of your life is spent working in your life; this time is for working on your life—which means you need to get away.

Practical Help: it doesn't have to be expensive! It could be a friend's spare bedroom in another city, a cheap hotel, or a friend's cabin. We never spend much money on a "WE" Retreat, mainly because the focus of our time is each other, not the beach.

What do we need to take?
- Both guidebooks—one for him and one for her
- Pens
- Wifi to watch videos (or download)

Everything you need to complete the work described in the Fruitful Marriage Video Series is here in this guidebook.

PRO TIPS

Be brutally honest, gently.
I (Josh) don't have a problem being brutally honest. It was the gently part I had to work on. Early in our marriage, Sharon often misread my intensity in tackling a challenge as attacking her instead. My enthusiasm to solve a problem became the problem.

Conversely, I (Sharon) would sometimes struggle saying what I really thought because I didn't want to hurt Josh's feelings. My timidity sometimes led me to hold back, which meant I wasn't sharing the whole truth.

Neither of these extremes is helpful. Be loving. Be gracious. Be kind. And be honest, gently.

Resolve to tackle the hard things.
Don't ignore the sucking chest wound. That won't help anything. If it helps to start with some easier topics and get a few wins under your belt, go for it! Sometimes it can feel good to build some momentum knocking-out a couple easy targets first. But don't dance around the hard issues for too long. Resolve to get to them. The more you put them off, the more they'll hurt your marriage. We encourage taking them head on.

This isn't about winning; it's about uniting.
The goal is to get on the same page, not win an argument. Don't make it your goal to always get your way. Remember, you're there as a team, tackling challenges together. Keep that as your target. Your spouse is not the enemy. If you have frustrations, speak them gently. If your spouse has frustrations, receive them humbly. Don't see each other as the problem. Get shoulder to shoulder and together face the problem. Remember, your spouse has gifts you don't and a perspective that you need. Ask questions, talk less, listen more. Work as a team.

Ask people you trust to pray for you.
Why not? Invite them into the process. Give them as many specifics as you'd like. Ask them to pray at certain times or whenever the Lord brings you to mind. What could be better than people you love praying for your success on the 3-5 most important days of your year? Satan won't like what you're doing and will most likely attack with distraction or discouragement. Punch back with prayer.

Make sure you allow plenty of time for fun.
Sharon and I use the 3 P's to guide our time. Pray together. Plan together. Play together. Go for walks. Work out. Explore. Go for a drive. Ski. Catch a show. Attend a concert. Eat good food. Sleep in. Do whatever energizes you. Your brain needs time and space.

You might have some of your best ideas while you're having fun. Give yourself 4-6 hours a day to really crank, then unplug the rest of the day and have fun. Morning couple? Perfect. Crank in the morning and when noon hits, it's party time!

Don't be discouraged if you don't get to everything.
I (Sharon) can easily get overwhelmed by it all, or frustrated if I can't check all the boxes. Take a deep breath. Sometimes a specific topic or problem will take longer to work through than you planned. Don't lose heart. If you get stuck, take a break. Pray and ask for wisdom. Go get tacos. Make love. And then come back to it. And if you don't get all the problems worked out this time, at least get to a place where you both feel comfortable. That's why you have multiple days and why you should get away multiple times every year!

PRACTICAL ENCOURAGEMENT FOR MOMS

From Sharon

Mommas, dear mommas. Some of you are thinking, "Did he say 3-5 days? How can I leave my kids for so long? What will they do without me?" Let me remind you, dear friends, your marriage is a higher priority than your sweet little people. In fact, your relationship with your husband is your number one priority after your relationship with Christ. And I completely agree with what my man said earlier: one of the ways you as a mom model this for your kids is by getting away with just dad!

So how do you do this practically? Here are a couple of things I have done in years past to help me take off my "mom hat" and focus on my primary role as wife to Josh while we are away.

Find solid babysitting. Make sure you have someone taking care of your children who you trust implicitly. The goal is for you to unplug completely and not have to constantly check back in (Did they change Johnny's diaper on time? Did Susie drink her milk? Did they give them their favorite blankie for bed?). You've hired them for this job, now let them do it.

Leave a schedule. Feel free to type out a schedule and list the things your babysitter needs to know! Think through specifics and then put it all in one place. Each time we went away for a weekend, we left two able-bodied kids and two physically-handicapped kids who needed specific care, scheduled medications, and someone who could spot warning signs if their medically-implanted equipment malfunctioned. It helped me immensely to type out every little detail. A schedule allowed my mind to be free to enjoy the weekend, while providing instruction for the caregivers so they wouldn't need to check in, unless it was an emergency.

Have your husband handle goodbyes. Be the first one in the car, not the last. This was especially helpful when our kids were small. Before we left for our weekend, we would gather as a family and pray together and Josh would explain to the kids what we were going to be doing while we were away. He would also give them directions regarding their behavior and how they could be praying for us. Then I would give hugs and get in the truck. He would be the last one to say goodbye and if any were in tears, he would comfort and help them before he came out to join me. This helped tremendously. It took the pressure off of me to not have to peel a child away while they cried. Instead, this allowed me a quiet, three minutes in the truck to take a deep breath and take the "mom hat" off.

Choose to engage your mind. Taking off said "mom hat" is a choice. If you continue to worry and fret about the children and the home, whether verbally or in your mind, you will neutralize your weekend. By choosing to dwell on the secondary priorities (your children) that you have left at home, you will be actively ignoring and neglecting your primary priority (your husband). And let me tell you, if you do this, he will be frustrated and you will be exhausted.

Ask the Lord to help you trust Him. Leaving your children at home and focusing on your marriage for a couple of days will be, for some of you, a lesson in trust. If you have secured solid babysitting, left detailed instructions, and have made your way out of the house, the next step for you is to trust. Trust that God is sovereign over all and loves your children more than you. No, really. He does.

If you are prone to worry and control, especially when it comes to your children, you will need to ask the Lord for help in this area. Have some close friends pray for you about this. Tell your husband and ask him to pray over you and the weekend. In the days leading up to the weekend, fill your mind with the truth of God's Word about who He is and His control over all things. And then watch in awe as you prioritize this God-designed institution of marriage, for you will see and reap benefits far beyond your imagination. He can be trusted, and you can do this!

OUR PRAYER FOR YOU

Sharon and I are very aware that many of you are coming from different walks and stages in life. If you are like we frequently find ourselves, you may be coming to this book tired and a little beat up by life.

We don't want to assume that we're all starting from the same place. So here's a quick assessment to let you know that we acknowledge there are different starting points for each of us, and we want to identify them and speak to them. Where would you say you're at right now?

Maybe your marriage is doing great and going strong. But some things have changed and you need to make adjustments. We're praying that this "WE" Retreat would help you move towards more order and peace.

Maybe you're feeling stale and stuck. We're praying that God gives you a breakthrough and helps you make progress. Sometimes it's just a spark that helps you get unstuck from 5 or 30 years in a rut.

Maybe your marriage is dysfunctional and exhausting. We're praying in Jesus' name that you move towards health, individually and as a couple.

You may be in a marriage that's abusive and harmful. What you need is deliverance and freedom. If you are a husband who is spiritually, emotionally, sexually, and/or physically abusive, our prayer is that God would put His foot on your throat to awaken your need to repent. God hates men who use their power to abuse women.

You may be in a marriage with a wife who's emotionally manipulative. We're praying that your marriage would be delivered from that through repentance and that both you and your spouse would experience freedom from passive-aggressive, manipulative ways.

Maybe your marriage is broken and battered. We're praying that you'll find healing and wholeness.

Maybe you're just plain busy and tired. We're praying that the Lord would use this time away from the hustle-and-bustle to help bring order and peace. And we want to be clear when we say this—even a highly fruitful "WE" Retreat won't be a one-time fix. It's not like Sharon and I figured it out 23 years ago and it's been clear sailing all along. We've have to make changes and adjustments in each new season of life. So hang in there for the long haul.

Maybe your marriage has been distracted and neglected. We're praying that God would grant you focused attention to give to your marriage clarity you have never had before.

Maybe your marriage is ignorant and immature. You just don't know what you don't know. Maybe you're new to the faith or you've been walking with Jesus for a while, but you've been disobedient to keep growing and learning. We're praying that God would give you wisdom so you can move towards maturity together. There is no maturity without wisdom, and wisdom begins with the fear of God.

We know there are some marriages that need more help than what any book can give. Your marriage may need deep intervention and intensives. But here's what we do know—if you humble yourselves, if you confess your sin to one another, if you ask for help, if you put the needs of your spouse ahead of your own, if you take responsibility for your own sin and stop blaming other people for what you yourself have done, and if you actually invest your focused time and energy to farming your "WE," you will find your marriage stronger. That's our hope, that's our prayer for you all.

PRE "WE" RETREAT ASSIGNMENT
Complete individually, then read to each other.
EST. 10 MINUTES

What am I hoping to get out of this weekend?

What is the biggest hindrance that could get in the way?

ON YOUR "WE" RETREAT

CHAPTER 1
COVENANT

Covenant is the Seed of your "WE" Tree

WATCH VIDEO SESSION 1

THE "WE" TREE

STRANDS OF COVENANT DNA

1. Relational Stability

2. Personal Sanctification

8. Marital Success

3. Emotional Safety

7. External Significance

COVENANT is the Seed

4. Sexual Satisfaction

6. Exponential Strength

5. Generational Seed

We pray you'll experience the POWER, the PRIVILEGE, the PASSION, and the PLEASURE that can only be found within covenant marriage.

NOTES

MARRIAGE ASSESSMENT
EST. 20 MINUTES

What do I really enjoy about our relationship?

What do I need to work on / address in my own life?

What do WE need to work on / address as a couple?

What conflict needs to be resolved? What are areas of disagreement or stress?

What areas need to be discussed or decisions need to be made?

How would I rate our **physical** intimacy and closeness?

Less intimate									More intimate
1	2	3	4	5	6	7	8	9	10

How would I rate our **spiritual** intimacy and closeness?

Less intimate									More intimate
1	2	3	4	5	6	7	8	9	10

How would I rate our **emotional** intimacy and closeness?

Less intimate									More intimate
1	2	3	4	5	6	7	8	9	10

What are 5 words I would use to describe our marriage?

#1

#2

#3

#4

#5

CHAPTER 1 | ASSIGNMENTS

AFFIRMATION EXERCISE
Complete individually, then read to each other.
EST. 30 MINUTES

Write 5 things you appreciate about your husband.

1.

2.

3.

4.

5.

CHAPTER 1 | ASSIGNMENTS

Write 5 ways you see God working in your husband's life.

1.

2.

3.

4.

5.

TAKE A BREAK

**Well Done. Congratulations!
Time to take a break!**

**Take a walk. Watch a movie.
Rub each other's feet.
Get a nice dinner. Go!**

CHAPTER 2
VALUES

Values are the unseen Roots of your "WE" Tree

WATCH VIDEO SESSION 2

Where It All Starts
The unseen roots determine the health of the visible tree. So too, our unseen values determine the health of our visible relationships. Buried under the surface, values serve to feed and nurture the "WE" Tree above the surface.

Roots as a Delivery System
Values serve to guide our everyday decisions. What do you value? What do We value? What things are most important to us? What will guide and anchor us? Are our values consistent with God's values? What needs to be added? Changed? Strengthened? Values are what determine your everyday actions, and yet few of us have actually thought about them.

Roots as an Anchor
Roots anchor a tree to the soil. For Christians, this soil is the Word of God. We want our life anchored deeply in the Word of God. We want our values drawing nutrients from the life-giving, divine revelation of God's Holy Word. We want the good soil of God's Word informing and shaping of the values that feed our marriage. Reading the verses on **page** 25 for a biblical framework will be a good place to start.

Two kinds of Values
Aspirational values are like goals (diet and exercise). Actual values are measured by ongoing behavior (ice cream and couch). Certainly, these can be measured in degrees, but unless a value is demonstrated in consistent behavior, it isn't actual. If you say you value communication with your spouse, but they say you value scrolling on your phone, your aspirational versus actual values are in conflict. And it's easy to deceive yourself into believing you're doing better than you actually are. This is why you need to ask someone close and trusted (like your spouse) to tell you if what you say you value is actually true.

Three Sources of Values
1. Self

2. Satan

3. Scripture

Personal (ME) Values —vs— "WE" Values
To get to your "WE" Tree, you need to start with your individual values. Do they feed the strength of your "WE" values or compete with, or even take away from them? Once you've identified your individual values, then you can begin identifying and articulating your "WE" values.

Target Values
The purpose of this exercise is to articulate your aspirational values. What are those things you will choose to make most important in your life and marriage? Then use those to evaluate your actual values and see where you need to change, repent, and grow. These articulated values now give you something to live into.

Write, Read, Reflect, Tweak
Start by putting down what immediately comes to mind. What do you value? What's most important to you? It can be a word or a phrase. When done, read the selected Bible verses. Reflect on your values. What needs to change? Upon reflection, make any necessary adjustments. Follow the same process for your "WE" values.

Share & Build
Upon completion, share your individual values with your spouse. Use the opportunity to get input. Do you see me living these out? Next, have your spouse share their values. Once you've shared both your lists, work at assimilating them together to build a comprehensive "WE" values list. This list can be tweaked, adjusted, and added to year after year.

NOTES

CHAPTER 2 | ASSIGNMENTS

INDIVIDUAL VALUES
Complete individually, then share with each other.
EST. 30-60 MINUTES

Example Values For A Wife
"I value giving in such a way that surprises and blesses others."
"I value learning."

"WE" VALUES
EST. 30-60 MINUTES

Example "WE" Values For a Couple
"We value fighting for unity."
"We value intimacy."
"We value hospitality."

CHAPTER 2 | ASSIGNMENTS

CHAPTER 2 | ASSIGNMENTS

"WE" VALUES
(Additional space, if needed)

TAKE A BREAK

**You're doing great. Keep going!
Time for more fun!**

**Renew your covenant (seriously!).
Go get some fresh air. Grab a snack.
Get something to drink.**

CHAPTER 3

VISION

Vision is the Trunk of your "WE" Tree

WATCH VIDEO SESSION 3

MARRIAGE VISION

"LOOK CAREFULLY then how you walk, not as unwise but as wise, making the most of every opportunity, because the days are evil."
Ephesians 5:15-16

The Bible is clear: if you don't pay attention to your life, you will wander off course. The same is true of your marriage. Without vision, people stumble. Without a crystal-clear vision guiding and governing, pulling and pushing, protecting and compelling, and continually uniting and binding you and your spouse together, one of two things will happen: 1) you'll drift apart from each other, or 2) together, you'll drift apart from God. Neither are good options. So let's look carefully then how we live.

The Bible is also clear: God has given us opportunities. Your job is to make the most of them. Your marriage is one of the greatest opportunities God's given you. It contains the potential for life, heritage, pleasure, happiness, contentment, meaning, purpose, power, grace, forgiveness, revelation, learning, discovery, growth, and the ability to bless the world long after you're gone through leaving a generational legacy. Your marriage has the most potential to make the biggest impact out of anything in your life.

If you want to be a wise person who makes the best use of their days and opportunities, the place to start is getting a vision for your marriage.

NOTES

NOTES

START HERE

Pray Together...Ask the Lord for help. Thank Him for helping you get clarity in the assessment. Thank Him for what He's brought you through and healed you from. Ask Him to speak to you, lead you, guide you. Tell Him you're listening.

Consider...Look at your assessments. If you were to continue down certain paths where there is current conflict or lack of clarity, what might that result in? What regrets are you unwilling to live with?

Review...Read your values out loud to each other, both your personal values and your "WE" Values. Have them in your heart as context for building your marriage vision.

Cherry Pick...Are there any key or repeated themes that jump out as you review your values? If so, how might you include those in your vision statements?

Imagine...What kind of words do you want people to use to describe your marriage, family, and legacy?

Refine...The goal is a compelling statement (or two) that stirs your hearts. And the best vision statements are often the shortest. So get all sorts of ideas down and then ruthlessly cut until it is sharp, simple, and penetrating.

BIG PICTURE

Complete individually, then share with each other.

EST. 30-60 MINUTES

State why God has put us together.

Name things we know God has called us to do.

What are things we (as a couple or family) are mutually passionate about and gifted at?

Name three ways I would want someone to describe the culture of our home.

What do we sense God calling us to do for Him this year? What would be a strategic, short-term vision for our marriage? (How should we use our time, resources, wealth, knowledge, relationships, passions, and giftings to further His Kingdom? What strategic points of growth and specific areas should we focus on given our season of life?)

CHAPTER 3 | ASSIGNMENTS

YOUR MARRIAGE LEGACY
Work on this with your husband.
EST. 20 MINUTES

Imagine you and your spouse died together, holding hands, sitting on the front porch, on your 60th wedding anniversary (one can dream!). What do you hope is said about you? Write your obituary. Use the space below or a word doc.

(Example: Josh and Sharon were quite the pair. He loved to make her laugh. She loved to make him blush. Their home was always open, and more than one person reported a life-changing experience while sitting next to their fire. They loved hospitality and sharing what they had with others. Known for their relentless commitment to Jesus, His Church, their family, and the valley they called home, their passion and relentless work ethic strengthened countless marriages and families. Their children grew up knowing they were loved and laughing a lot. All four children have a personal relationship with Jesus, love the Church, and are guided by a deep sense of values they absorbed from the atmosphere of their home. As a wife, Sharon was known for...)

YOUR MARRIAGE VISION
Work on this with your husband.
EST. 60 MINUTES

This is the culmination of all our work to-date. Values are who you want to be, but vision is where you want to go. This is a compelling articulation of a preferred future together. Don't cut corners. Dream big. There's power in speaking it, writing it, and believing it. This is the target you aim at. The flag you climb towards. The purpose you live for. Write it in present-tense reality, as what you want to be true of your marriage in 20 years. Include key Scriptures if you'd like. Try to keep it short and clearly defined.

YOUR MARRIAGE VISION
(Additional space, if needed)

TAKE A BREAK

**Great work. Don't stop now!
But you deserve a break.**

**Renew that covenant again!
Maybe it's time for lunch? Drink some
kombucha, eat some kale or tri-tip...whatever
blows your hair back.**

CHAPTER 4
AGREEMENTS

Agreements are the **Branches** of your "WE" Tree

WATCH VIDEO SESSION 4

Agreements are the Branches, the practical outworking of the marriage vision. Agreements are what unity grows on.

Four Branch Facts
1. Branches are the distribution system connecting roots to fruit. The top of the tree requires the bottom of the tree to perform well, and vice-versa.

2. Branches grow naturally to balance the tree and fill space for growing fruit.

3. Young branches must often be gently guided to grow properly.

4. A strategically pruned branch increases a tree's vigor; a randomly broken branch hurts a tree's vigor.

Building Agreements = "WE" Superpower

CHAPTER 4 | VIDEO SESSION

Two Promises of Agreements
1. Direction
2. Unity

Three Principles of Agreement-Building

1. It's not about getting **your** way but finding **God's** way.

2. It's not about negotiating but **serving**...not about demanding **sacrificing**...not about winning but **uniting**.

3. It's not about lose-lose or win-lose but **win-win**.

Three Kinds of Agreements
1. **Bad** Agreement i.e. "We don't talk about that."
2. **Broken** Agreement i.e. "I don't trust him."
3. **Built** Agreement i.e. "We're on the same page."

CHAPTER 4 | VIDEO SESSION

Three Reasons Building Agreements is Hard For Men
1. You're Involved
2. Humility is Involved
3. Listening is Involved

Three Reasons Building Agreements is Hard For Women
1. You're Involved
2. Humility is Involved
3. Listening is Involved

**The opposite of an agreement is an assumption.
Assumptions are landmines in relationships.**

CHAPTER 4 | VIDEO SESSION

Two Mindsets of Agreements
1. "WE" are a team.
2. This is good for me, because "me" = "WE."

Two Postures for Building Agreements
1. Openness before God.
2. Respect towards your spouse.

CHAPTER 4 | VIDEO SESSION

Seven Practices of Building Agreements

1. Start with prayer.

2. State the problem.

3. Share your ideas.

4. Seek wise counsel.

5. Scan your Values and Vision.

6. Set it aside (when feeling stuck, it's okay to hit pause and return later).

7. Solidify your Agreements.

NOTES

CHAPTER 4 | ASSIGNMENT

AREAS FOR AGREEMENTS

Take five minutes to jot down some areas in your life where you think agreements would be helpful.

TAKE A BREAK

**Good job getting through those 2 sessions.
Quick break.**

**Jump up and down.
Do 5 burpees.
Stretch. Touch your toes.
Keep going!**

CHAPTER 5
UNITY & ONENESS
Unity and Oneness are the **Leaves** and **Fruit** of your "We" Tree

WATCH VIDEO SESSION 5

Unity is the **Leaf** that energizes and protects your marriage.

Four Fun Facts About Leaves
1. Leaves are mini solar panels converting light into energy.

2. Leaves are the factory that converts energy into chemical food for the Tree to eat.

3. If a Tree didn't have leaves, the sun wouldn't matter.

4. Leaves tell you everything you need to know about a Tree's vigor and turgor.

Four Principles of Unity
1. God loves unity.

2. Satan loves division.

3. Unity in marriage occurs when living for something bigger than the marriage.

4. Unity requires hard work and vigilance. It is forged and fought for, not fallen into.

Unity is the high ground of spiritual warfare in marriage. Hold it at any cost.

CHAPTER 5 | VIDEO SESSION

Four Promises of Unity
1. Unlimited Potential

2. Supernatural Blessing

3. Supernatural Power

4. Answered Prayer

Four Prerequisites of Unity
1. Walk in the Spirit not the Flesh (Galatians 5:17-24)

2. Practice repentance, not defensiveness (Ephesians 4:25-27)

3. Submit to Authority (Ephesians 5:21)

4. Extend forgiveness when needed (Ephesians 4:26-32)

Oneness is the **Fruit** that grows in the marriage.

Three Realities of Oneness
1. Oneness is a gift Gift; you don't make it, God gives it.

2. Oneness is Dynamic; it requires constant attention

3. It must be Farmed; your job is to care for the Tree

NOTES

CHAPTER 5 | ASSIGNMENT

REVIEW THE 6 CRITICAL ELEMENTS FOR A GODLY MARRIAGE

(See Appendix B)

EST. 20 MINUTES

1. God's Word is the Soil.

2. Holy Spirit is the Water.

3. Affirmation is the Nutrition.

4. Grace is the Climate.

5. Trust is the Environment.

6. Love is the Sun.

TAKE A BREAK

You're crushing it! Only one more session to go!

**Drink some more water. Get some food.
Take a few laps around the building.
Give your spouse a big smooch.
Now back to it!**

CHAPTER 6
BUILDING AGREEMENTS

AGREEMENT PRO TIPS

"Do two walk together unless they have agreed to do so?"
Amos 3:3

I (Sharon) love agreements. They bring so much confidence to me as a wife and mother. When Josh and I make an agreement in a certain area of our marriage, it provides direction and clarity. It's amazing! And it makes a direct impact daily on the health of our "WE."

We suggest that before you begin hammering out and articulating your agreements, you first take time to quickly review your "WE" Values that you wrote down on day two and your "WE" Vision from day three. Values are the roots that feed the life of the tree (who "WE" want to be), Vision is the trunk that serves as the backbone of the tree (where "WE" want to go), Agreements are the branches growing out of the trunk (how "WE" will live) upon which Unity and Oneness will grow. Reviewing these will help you focus in on what you want to be about as a couple.

From there, you can build agreements that will help you actually be that couple.

Some agreements will be specific to challenges you're facing, some will address unique circumstances, some will be ways to combat sin, some will be practical in nature, some will be situationally specific. The point...you build them together.

As you start this process of building agreements, here's a few things to keep in mind:

Pray. Ask the Lord to give you wisdom and insight in order to integrate your values and vision in a way that results in concrete, wise, practical agreements. Ask specifically for the Lord to 1) keep you humble, 2) give you wisdom, 3) help you walk in the fruits of the Spirit, 4) give you eyes to see the value your spouse brings, 5) unify your hearts together through this process.

Start with the most distinct areas first. Review your "WE" Tree Rapid Assessment, look at the three lowest scores, and start there. Do you have agreements already in place? If so, which ones need to go (prune)? Which ones need to change (graft)? What do you need to add (grow)?

As you go through each area of your assessment, discuss what the hotspots are in that part of your marriage. Do you often bicker about finances? Are you frustrated because people show up at your house after your spouse invited them without asking you? Are you tired of your spouse correcting you in front of the kids? Do you often argue about your in-laws? These are where you need unity. These are the areas for which you must build agreements.

Make them simple, specific, and personal. Don't overcomplicate them. Don't be vague or generic. This will only bring more confusion. Articulate them clearly.

Make adjustments, as needed. Agreements should be discussed for effectiveness as time goes on. You may need to adjust some specifically as kids get older, parents age, or vocations change.

Be honest. You must both share openly and honestly. The goal is to have both perspectives baked into each agreement. This is what makes them strong! I (Sharon) often needed to be reminded early in our marriage that Josh is not a mind-reader. I had to learn to say what I was thinking and be honest. As he graciously reminded me, I was robbing our marriage of my wisdom and failing in my role as helper when I was timid or held back my perspective.

Be agreeable. Agreements are not one person pushing their agenda or desires until the other one gives up. It is not an agreement until both of you, well, agree. And while concessions are good, caving is not. Both voices should be voiced, heard, and understood until an agreement is reached that you both can fully support. This might result in some arguing. That's OK! Fight fair. Stay humble. Don't leave the table. Stay at it. Commit to finish. Better a few days arguing and year of peace than a few days avoiding hard topics and a year of division and hell. And remember, the agreements forged in fire are the strongest agreements that will hold in the hardest of times!

Stick to them. Once you've agreed to it, do it! Remember, agreements are the branches of your "WE" Tree. If you break an agreement that you and your spouse built, you are not just hurting your spouse, you are hurting the "WE," which means you too. It is damage that will take time to heal and trust that will have to be restored. If you mess up, then repent, forgive, and review your agreement to make sure it is still what you both think is best. Remember, these agreements are for your good!

Give it time. If this is your first attempt at building agreements, be patient! With practice, work, and humility, building agreements gets easier and more intuitive. Before you know it, you will find yourself moving more and more in sync as a couple, like a basketball team that's played so much together they can pass without looking and know the other will be there. Agreements will be so intuitive that it would feel unnatural and weird to make a decision without your spouse. And if you have to make a decision without them, you've spent so much time listening to them that you can make a decision with them in mind that still protects your "WE." Agreements are a beautiful thing. The more you have, the stronger your "WE."

BUILDING AGREEMENTS

The following are key areas every couple needs agreements for. The agreements you build should be practical ways you can live out your values and live towards your vision. There are no limits to the number of agreements you can make for each category. They should be specific to your story, shore up your weaknesses, protect your vulnerabilities, and speak to your needs.

EST. 30-60 MINUTES

Agreement Category: Finances

Examples: We agree not to purchase something that costs over $50 without talking to each other first / We agree that generosity to our home church is priority over personal indulgence / We agree to put away 15% every month for financial freedom later / We agree Josh will manage overall vision and Sharon will manage day to day finances / etc., etc.

Agreement Category: In-laws

Examples: We agree to do whatever it takes to make each other feel prioritized over the other's family / We agree to find ways to meaningfully involve aunts and uncles, grandpas and grandmas, in our children's life for the sake of influence / etc., etc.

Agreement Category: Friendships

Examples: We agree to not pursue one-on-one friendships with members of the opposite sex outside the context of husband-wife friends—this includes social media, texting, calling, or "hanging out" / We agree to let the other sign off on friends and allow the other's discernment to protect us from things we might not see / We agree to serve and love everyone, but choose to be friends with a few / etc., etc.

CHAPTER 6 | ASSIGNMENTS

Agreement Category: TV / Devices / Screens

Examples: We won't watch TV in the middle of the day / We agree our kids will never watch something we haven't seen first / We agree the TV will not take a central place in our home / We agree we won't have a TV in our bedroom / etc., etc.

Agreement Category: Parenting (discipline, schedule, roles)

Examples: We agree that when frustrated we will not disagree with or contradict the other in front of our kids / We agree to support the other publicly and discuss differences in private / etc., etc.

BUILDING AGREEMENTS (Continued)

Other categories where you may need to build agreements:
Holidays / Recreation / Fitness / Vocation / Hospitality / Home / Discipline /
Meals / Roles / Holidays and Traditions / Kids' education / Entertainment / Vacations

Agreement Category:

Agreement Category:

Agreement Category:

Agreement Category:

Agreement Category:

Agreement Category:

Agreement Category:

Agreement Category:

Agreement Category:

Agreement Category:

CHAPTER 6 | ASSIGNMENTS

AGREEMENT ACTION PLAN

The key to success is turning your agreements into action. Read through your new values and agreements and highlight anything that requires a change—or action step—when you get home in order to live it out. Changes may need to be made to your commitments, schedules, routines, habits, relationships, devices, etc.

EST. 30-60 MINUTES

Example
Agreement: We agree to not have screens in our bedroom.
Action Step: We will move the TV into the family room & leave phones in the kitchen.

Agreement

Action Step

Agreement

Action Step

Agreement

Action Step

Agreement

Action Step

CHAPTER 6 | ASSIGNMENTS

Agreement

Action Step

Agreement

Action Step

Agreement

Action Step

Agreement

Action Step

Agreement

Action Step

Congratulations!!!! You completed your first "WE" Retreat! The first is always the hardest.
You have taken a significant step towards power and wholeness in marriage. You are to be commended.
The work will be worth it!

NOW WHAT?

Before you leave

Journal
What did you learn? How did you grow? Where did you experience God work? What are you grateful for?

Pray
Thank the Lord for all He's done during your time away. Ask for His help as you move forward.

Schedule
Pick the date for your next "WE" Retreat.

After you get home

Capture
Type out your values, vision, and agreements so you have them in a document you can edit, add to, or print out.

Share
Read what you worked on to your kids. Share any new family mottos you came up with or new routines you will be implementing. Share with your small group, Bible study, close friends, other married couples, etc.

Review
Set aside regular "WE" Retreat Meetings to review your agreements and check how you're doing. This should be a time of accountability, but also encouragement!

We are so proud of you for putting in the hard work it took to finish this "WE" Retreat. We know it demanded a lot of energy and effort. Our prayer is that the Lord has used this weekend to grow your intimacy with Him and each other. Living out the vision and agreements you've hammered out will take patience and perseverance, but the fruit will be worth it. We love you and are cheering for you.

Now pull up your boots and go Farm Your "WE!"

APPENDIX

APPENDIX A
BIBLE VERSES TO FEED YOUR ROOTS

Deuteronomy 6:4-5
4 Hear, O Israel: The Lord our God, the Lord is one. 5 Love the Lord your God with all your heart and with all your soul and with all your strength. 6 These commandments that I give you today are to be on your hearts.

John 14:21
Whoever has my commands and keeps them is the one who loves me. The one who loves me will be loved by my Father, and I too will love them and show myself to them."

Romans 8:1-14
Therefore, there is now no condemnation for those who are in Christ Jesus…

5 Those who live according to the flesh have their minds set on what the flesh desires; but those who live in accordance with the Spirit have their minds set on what the Spirit desires. 6 The mind governed by the flesh is death, but the mind governed by the Spirit is life and peace. 7 The mind governed by the flesh is hostile to God; it does not submit to God's law, nor can it do so. 8 Those who are in the realm of the flesh cannot please God.
9 You, however, are not in the realm of the flesh but are in the realm of the Spirit, if indeed the Spirit of God lives in you. And if anyone does not have the Spirit of Christ, they do not belong to Christ. 10 But if Christ is in you, then even though your body is subject to death because of sin, the Spirit gives life because of righteousness. 11 And if the Spirit of him who raised Jesus from the dead is living in you, he who raised Christ from the dead will also give life to your mortal bodies because of his Spirit who lives in you.
12 Therefore, brothers and sisters, we have an obligation—but it is not to the flesh, to live according to it. 13 For if you live according to the flesh, you will die; but if by the Spirit you put to death the misdeeds of the body, you will live.
14 For those who are led by the Spirit of God are the children of God.

Galatians 6:7-10
Do not be deceived: God cannot be mocked. A man reaps what he sows. 8 Whoever sows to please their flesh, from the flesh will reap destruction; whoever sows to please the Spirit, from the Spirit will reap eternal life. 9 Let us not become weary in doing good, for at the proper time we will reap a harvest if we do not give up. 10 Therefore, as we have opportunity, let us do good to all people, especially to those who belong to the family of believers.

APPENDIX B
6 CRITICAL ELEMENTS OF A GODLY MARRIAGE
Your "WE" Tree can't thrive without these!

God's Word is the Soil
that keeps the "WE" Tree nutrified and anchored.

Your values, those unseen roots, draw nutrients from and are anchored by some kind of soil. As we shared in Chapter 2, your values will always be drawn from one of three sources: yourselves, Satan, or the Holy Word of God. It's our hope and prayer that your "WE" Tree would be firmly rooted in the truth and love of God.

See page 25 for a sample of key, nutrient-rich verses on marriage and a note on our DIGGING DEEP: Bible Verses to Feed Your "WE" Tree's Roots resource, available online.

Are you feeling stuck on a decision that needs to be made or a conversation that needs to be started? Or maybe you're just struggling to put words to your values and your vision? Output problems are often indicative of input problems. We encourage you to dive deep into God's Word to help you see your marriage through His eyes.

Holy Spirit is the Water
that keeps the "WE" Tree invigorated.

Fun Facts About Water in Relationship to Trees
Trees are 80% water. That means 80% of what you see above the ground is water. So, too, the Holy Spirit should be visible in 80% of your marriage. None of us can walk in the Spirit perfectly, and there's grace for that, but without the Holy Spirit (without water), our "WE" Trees would wither and die.

Water that serves a tree comes from the holding tank of the soil. Rain does not directly sustain a tree. It requires good soil to hold it and make it accessible in times of need. Good soil holds water. Bad soil does not. Your marriage's "WE" Tree will be radically healthier when you are tapping into the power of the Holy Spirit like a reservoir of life working in concert with the holding tank of God's Word.

Water serves as the conduit delivering nutrients from the soil to needs of the tree. When a branch or a leaf or growing fruit needs a nutrient, it sends a message down the tree. And the only way the tree can get the required nutrition to that area is through the conduit of water within the tree. Water is quite literally the lifeblood of the tree, serving all parts of the tree with everything needed from the soil. So, too, in your marriage, the Holy Spirit functions to take the Word of God and connect it to your need.

> "You need the Word of God combined with the Spirit of God, and THAT is where the power is."
> ~ Pastor Josh

Affirmation is the Nutrition
that we apply to help the "WE" Tree grow.

A Lesson We Learned Growing Fruit Trees:
A few years back, we decided to plant some peach and nectarine and apricot trees at our home. We didn't know how to do that...as you'll see in a moment...so we brought in a dear friend who's an expert in this area. She connected us with excellent root stock, came to our home, and helped us plant the trees. That same week, she planted trees at her home. "Don't forget to follow the schedule to put triple 16 around the trunks," she told us. And then life got busy and our trees seemed to be growing and time flew by. Two years later, we visited this friend's home and began admiring some massive peach trees. "Wow, these are incredible! How long have these been growing?" we asked. "Two years ago," she replied. "Same as yours. Why, are yours not as big?" Sharon and I looked at each other and burst out laughing. Friends, we learned an important lesson that day. Triple 16 matters.

Affirmation in our marriages is like fertilizer—that extra source of nutrition we can apply to support the overall health and growth of a "WE" Tree. Affirmation causes a husband and a wife to flourish in different ways. When affirmation flows from a man to a women, it creates a needed sense of safety, security, and love. That brings comfort. When affirmation flows from a woman to a man, it creates that needed sense of identity, honor, and respect. That breeds courage.

Men need to be told that they have what it takes.
Women need to be told they'll be taken care of.

The Power of Affirmation
Affirmation builds relational capital.
Affirmation makes us emotionally accessible.
Affirmation creates emotional resilience.
Affirmation builds emotional connection.
Affirmation leads to a deeper sense of belonging.
Affirmation grows the work of God in the other.

As a final note on the power of affirmation, we want to share this axiom of truth: what you affirm multiplies and what you criticize metastasizes. Let that sink in. Our encouragement to you is to affirm each other often. Praise the ordinary, not just the exceptional. Be detailed and genuine. And watch your spouse flourish.

Grace is the Climate
needed for the "WE" Tree to thrive.

In our world, different climates—different weather patterns determined by latitude and longitude and elevation—determine how conducive it can be to grow a healthy, strong, fruit-bearing tree. In our marriages, it's grace that creates a relational climate in which a "WE" Tree can flourish.

DANGER: cold snaps.
In nature, a cold snap is a sudden onset of frigid air that is damaging to the health of a tree. So, too, record-keeping, or the keeping and weaponizing of past offenses, leads to discontentment and bitterness. It is a climate devoid of grace. Solution: remember the grace you've received from your Heavenly Father and apply that grace liberally to your spouse.

Where there are CHALLENGES, draw from God's grace to endure.

Where there are FAILURES, cover them with God's grace to heal.

Where there are VICTORIES, thank God for His grace in your lives.

Trust is the Environment
required for the "WE" Tree to breathe.

Trust is the currency of our relationships that we live on—the air in the environment we breathe. It's the foundation of our relationship with God, just as it is with every other relationship. The strength of each human relationship exists in direct proportion to our ability to trust that person. There can be no closeness, no intimacy, where there is no trust.

Because our Heavenly Father is infinitely trustworthy, our relationships with Him have unlimited capacity for depth and intimacy. As believers, you can draw on that trust and intimacy to create a healthy environment for your "WE" Tree.

Trust = Say + Do

Trust is based on doing what you say you'll do and then repeating that as a pattern over time. As actions align with words, over time, trust is established. As a currency, trust is earned in small amounts and lost in large amounts. Every word and interaction in your marriage will either make a deposit or a withdrawal.

When we trust someone, we open our heart to them. Put another way, being a trustworthy person allows others to feel safe and be vulnerable.

Environment Check
Ask yourself and then your spouse this question: am I a trustworthy person?

Love is the Sun
necessary for the "WE" Tree to live.

Take a moment to read 1 Corinthians 13 out loud.

We want to encourage you to learn how your spouse feels loved. This may be different from how you think they feel loved. Be prepared to be surprised. Take time right now to ask each other this question: what things do I do for you that make you feel most loved?

Here are example responses from our lives
Sharon: "I feel loved when you care for yourself physically. I fell loved because I want you to be around a long time to take care of me and the kids."
Josh: "I feel loved when you have a hot meal waiting for me when I get home. I feel loved because it shows me that you were looking forward to my return and anticipating it by doing something for me."

Sharon: "I feel loved when you fill up my gas tank the night before I go on a long trip."
Josh: "I feel loved when you listen to me talk."

Just as the sun gives power and energy to a tree, love fuels the vibrancy of your marriage. Love is so much more than a feeling. Love is a conscious choice and commitment to adhere to the marriage covenant.

Love shines on your "WE" Tree most fully when both individuals have laid aside their individual desires for the greater need of the "WE" Tree. We want to encourage you to this truth of marriage, that your "WE" is more important than your "me." There is a power in that type of self-sacrificial love that puts to death selfish needs in order to love and serve the needs of the marriage. When neither spouse is doing this, you get a dead tree. When one spouse is doing this but not the other, you get a lopsided, unhealthy tree. But when both are joyfully serving the other, you get a life-giving, fruit-bearing tree that will feed many for generations to come.

ADDITIONAL RESOURCES
Available at
www.StrongerManNation.com

www.ingramcontent.com/pod-product-compliance
Lightning Source LLC
Chambersburg PA
CBHW080547090426
42734CB00016B/3222